Safari Animals™
Animales de safari™

GIRAFFES
JIRAFAS

Amelie von Zumbusch

Traducción al español: Ma. Pilar Sanz

PowerKiDS press & **Editorial Buenas Letras**™

New York

Published in 2007 by The Rosen Publishing Group, Inc.
29 East 21st Street, New York, NY 10010

First Edition

Book Design: Erica Clendening
Layout Design: Julio Gil and Lissette González

Photo Credits: Cover, pp. 1, 5, 17, 23 © Artville; pp. 7, 13, 15, 19, 21, 24 (top left, top right, bottom right) © Digital Vision; pp. 9, 11, 24 (bottom left) © Digital Stock.

Cataloging Data

Zumbusch, Amelie von.
  Giraffes-Jirafas / Amelie von Zumbusch; traducción al español Ma. Pilar Sanz — 1st ed.
    p. cm. — (Safari animals-Animales de safari)
  Includes index.
  ISBN-13: 978-1-4042-7606-2 (library binding)
  ISBN-10: 1-4042-7606-8 (library binding)
  1. Giraffe—Juvenile literature. 2. Spanish language materials. I. Title.

Manufactured in the United States of America

CONTENTS

CONTENIDO

The tallest animal on Earth is the giraffe. Giraffes can be up to 18 feet (5.5 m) tall.

El animal más alto de la Tierra es la jirafa. Las jirafas pueden llegar a medir 18 pies (5.5 m) de altura.

5

Giraffes live on the grasslands of Africa.

Las jirafas viven en las praderas de África.

Giraffes have very long necks. They also have long legs.

Las jirafas tienen cuellos muy largos. También tienen patas muy largas.

9

Giraffes have patterns on their coats. Each giraffe has a different pattern.

Las jirafas tienen diseños en su pelaje. Cada jirafa tiene un diseño diferente.

11

Each giraffe has two small horns on its head. A giraffe's horns are covered with hair.

Las jirafas tienen dos cuernos pequeños en la cabeza. Los cuernos de las jirafas están cubiertos de pelo.

13

Giraffes eat leaves. Their long necks let them reach the high leaves on tall trees.

Las jirafas comen las hojas de los árboles. Las jirafas usan sus largos cuellos para alcanzar las hojas de los árboles más altos..

15

The leaves of the acacia
tree are the food giraffes
like best.

Las hojas de un árbol,
llamado acacia, son
la comida preferida de
las jirafas.

17

Giraffes get water from the leaves they eat. They also drink water from water holes.

Las jirafas obtienen agua de las hojas de los árboles. Las jirafas también beben agua de las charcas.

Giraffes move across the grasslands in small groups.

Las jirafas se mueven por las praderas en pequeños grupos.

A baby giraffe is called a calf. A giraffe calf is already 6 feet (2 m) tall when it is born.

A los bebés de las jirafas se les llama crías. Al nacer, las crías de las jirafas tienen 6 pies (2 m) de altura.

23

Words to Know / Palabras que debes saber

grasslands / (las) praderas

horns / (los) cuernos

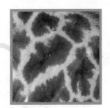

pattern / (el) diseño

water hole / (la) charca